Keep On Pressing

Rev. Dr. Michael D. Chaen

MESSAGES

FROM OUR

UNKNOWN ANCESTORS

A 31-Day Devotional Guided
By the Negro Spirituals

FOREWORD BY WILLIAM H. CURTIS

MICHAEL D. CHISM

Print ISBN: 978-1-54396-615-2

eBook ISBN: 978-1-54396-616-9

ACKNOWLEDGEMENTS

This book is dedicated to my Co-Mentors, Dr. William H. Curtis and Dr. Gina M. Stewart who didn't let me give up during my doctoral studies, my mother, who has always had my back, my family and friends who have always supported me and my children, who I love more than life itself.

TABLE OF CONTENTS

FOREWORD

I had the wonderful fortune of meeting Dr. Michael D. Chism when he enrolled as a Doctoral student at the United Theological Seminary in Dayton Ohio. I have been thankful to God for the privilege of being his Doctoral mentor every since. I discerned his deep devotional mind; His love for God; along with his deep and profound appreciation for the music of our African heritage. Theologian Soren Kierkegaard said, "Life can only be understood backwards, but it must be lived forward."

Dr. Chism, connects the history of African heritage conveyed in music and the forward spiritual journey we are all blessed to live. These devotions are deeply theological, scripturally accurate and very intimate in expression.

My morning devotions will be greatly enhanced with this resource and I pray it has wide reading and deep seeding for lives attempting to offer God faithful stewardship of mind, body and spirit.

Blessings,

Dr. William H. Curtis, Senior Pastor
Mount Ararat Baptist Church
Pgh. Pa

1

INTRODUCTION

I am my ancestor's wildest dreams. I believe my ancestors dreamt of a time when they would be free. I believe they dreamt of a time where they would be free to read and write and not be punished. It is my belief that they wanted to their voices to be heard. The Negro Spiritual was a vehicle that was used to bring the African American community to where it is today, telling of uprooted peoples' pain, sorrow, suffering but also providing hope to the singers and their listeners. Historically, they were sung in the fields among slaves and sharecroppers, in peoples' homes, and in churches. But in today's society, spirituals are seldom sung or even heard in churches due to the rise of hymns and mainstream gospel music. This devotional was written for several reasons. The first reason is that I believe we can still hear our ancestors' voices speaking through the music we listen to today. We can hear the call and response pattern, the syncopated rhythm, and other patterns which were birthed from the Negro Spirituals. The next reason is that although we are not times of slavery, we all go through tough, tumultuous times in our lives. We have worked from sun up to sundown. We have experienced our families being ripped apart at the seams. We've had to adapt to different cultures over time. We have felt like our deliverance is going to come. We have suffered at the expense of someone else and yet through it all, we have survived with the help of the Lord. The final reason for this devotional is that we can have hope. We can have hope trouble won't last always. We can know that nobody knows the trouble we've seen, nobody knows but Jesus. We can believe that soon we will be done with the troubles of this world because we will go home to be with God. The Negro Spirituals show us that we can look to God in our suffering. We can look to God in our oppression. We can look to God in our pain. Our conditions don't have to cause us to forget about God, but keep our eyes toward heaven. Our ancestors are still speaking and all we have to do is listen!

"SOON AH WILL BE DONE"

Day One

DEVOTION

There was a time I was laying in my room. I had just been punished because of my behavior in school. I laid there thinking, "There has to be more to life than this! No one should be treated this way!" One weekend, I attended a concert at one of the local African Methodist Episcopal Churches (I don't remember which one) and one of the songs in the concert was entitled, "Soon-A will Be Done." This song resonated in my spirit for several reasons. One reason is that it transported me to the mindset of our ancestors working from sun up to sundown for no pay, while being beaten for no reason at all. Cotton was being collected; the master's children were being cared for while their children were forced to work alongside them. The conditions were less than unfavorable, yet they had hope. Hope that one day things would change. Hope that one day things would be different. Hope that slavery would no longer be a part of their lives and one day they would be free. This is a time the slaves longed for!

This particular spiritual, like many others, is not ascribed to a specific author, although it was composed by William Dawson. This spiritual pointed toward a time where our ancestor would not have to deal with the troubles of the world. Our ancestors wanted to meet their mothers, possibly suggesting they never knew their mothers. But they knew they wanted to see Jesus, as referenced in the spiritual. Our ancestors knew their present reality wasn't their final destination and they looked forward to the time they would be able to go home to be with God. Our ancestors had hope despite the troubles they faced in the world.

We, just like our ancestors, do not have to mentally succumb to the troubles of this world. We, like our ancestors, can have hope despite the troubles we face.

WORDS FROM OUR ANCESTORS

Soon-A will be done with the trouble of this world. Soon-A will be done with the trouble of this world. Going home to live with God.

SCRIPTURE: 2 Corinthians 4:18(New International Version)

"THERE IS A BALM IN GILEAD"

Day Two

Our ancestors, according to Howard Thurman in his work Deep River: The Negro Spiritual Speaks of Life and Death, answered a question based on what they learned from the Holy Bible. Jeremiah 8:22 asked the question, "Is there no balm in Gilead?" Thurman says, "The basic insight here is one of optimism---an optimism that grows out of the pessimism of life and transcends it. It is an optimism that uses the pessimism of life as raw material out of which it creates its own strength." Our ancestor recognized there was an answer to this question. Thurman says, "The slave caught the mood of this spiritual dilemma, and with it an amazing thing. He straightened the question mark in Jeremiah's sentence into an exclamation point with an exclamation point: "There is a Balm in Gilead!"

Jeremiah knew the answer to his question as well, but the plight of the Israelites caused him to ask the question. We all deal with situations which cause us to ask questions, even if we know the answer. Our ancestors, in the dark moments of their lives knew there was a balm in Gilead. Our ancestors knew they had two answers to choose from in answering this age old question. Our ancestor could have been pessimistic in their approach and believed there was no Balm in Gilead, but decided to be optimistic and said there was a Balm in Gilead.

In our lives, we have to choose to either be pessimistic or optimistic. We can either see the glass half full or see the glass half empty. How we view the situations in our lives will determine how we handle our situations. If we see the glass half empty, we don't have hope that things will change. If we see the glass half full, we look forward to the day when things will change and do what we can until that day comes. An optimistic view about our situations gives us hope and gives us the push we need to deal with whatever life throws at us.

WORDS FROM OUR ANCESTORS

There is a balm in Gilead, to make the spirit whole. There is a balm in Gilead, to heal the sin-sick soul.

SCRIPTURE: Jeremiah 8:22 (New International Version)

"AIN'T DAT GOOD NEWS"

Day Three

DEVOTION

Isn't it a wonderful thing to receive some good news? I mean, it makes our heart skip a beat and we may even jump up and down for joy when we hear some good news. We may have been approved for a vehicle with no down payment and our monthly payments are low. We may have gotten approved for a house after living in a one bedroom apartment for the past few years. We could've gotten word our relative received a full scholarship to the college of their choice. All these situations are "Good News" situations.

Our unknown ancestors were working for free from sun up to sundown. Families were ripped apart, young children were forced to work in the fields at a young age. A slave who was there last night, wasn't there in the morning. Mother's were forced to carry the children of their masters after being raped. Trouble and turmoil was on every side, but in the midst of all of this, our unknown ancestors were able to find some good news.

How were they able to find good news when their families were being ripped apart? How were they able to find good news when they were beat by their masters so they could work harder? How were they able to find good news when they were taken from their homelands and forced to work for free? Our ancestors were able to find good news because they looked past their present reality. Our ancestors believed they had a home up in the kingdom, with God. Our ancestors believed their home was not on the plantation, but their home was in heaven with God. Our ancestors, although surrounded by what could be looked at as bad news, took the "Good News" they learned about and looked forward to that day.

We who are living in this 21st Century post-modern urban culture, can do the same. We may be surrounded by trouble. Our families may not be as close-knit as we would like them. We may work from sun up to sun down feeling like we are not paid what we are worth. But, there is "Good News" for those who believe in Jesus. The "Good News is that our home is not here, but our home is with the Lord. Ain't Dat Good News?!

WORDS FROM OUR ANCESTORS

I got a crown up-in-a-day kingdom Ain't Dat Good News. I got a crown up-in-a-day kingdom Ain't Dat Good News. I'm a gonna lay down this world, gonna shoulder up my cross. Gonna take it home to my Jesus, ain't dat good news.

SCRIPTURE: Proverbs 25:25(New International Version)

"EV'RY TIME I FEEL THE SPIRIT"

Day Four

DEVOTION

I was taught from a very young age, "Don't forget where you come from," or in other words, "Don't forget your roots." Your roots are what ground you. Your roots are what give you stability. Your roots give you what is necessary to make it in the world. I have visited several states in my lifetime, so far. Each state has its own culture and custom. I may call it soda in Philadelphia, but in Wilberforce Ohio, they call it "Pop." Now, while I was in Ohio, I started calling soda "Pop" because I had spent a considerable amount of time around persons living there, but I didn't forget that I learned that it was called soda.

Our unknown ancestors didn't forget their roots either. Our ancestors were from the Western coast of Africa and when they were brought to America, they were stripped of their customs and culture. Our ancestors were stripped of their tribal practices and ceremonies. The one thing that could not be stripped from them was music. Arthur C. Jones in his work Wade in the Water: the wisdom of the spirituals writes, "In their singing and praying, worshipers embraced selectively those aspects of Christianity that were in harmony with their intuitive African frame of reference; even when they lost knowledge of specific tribal practices and ceremonies, they maintained a basic African world view, which was difficult to eradicate. He further states, "Singing and dancing in the ring shout, participants entered into an altered state, much like their West African ancestors. The singing of the spirituals in the sacred circle of the ring shout provided an ideal setting for the emergence of spirit possession. It offered the individual and the witnessing community meaningful religious experiences in which the participants consistently felt the presence, support and direction of the divine spirit."

We are living in an age where things are changing daily. Apps on our phones or tablets are always updating. What may have looked one way yesterday doesn't look the same today. Fashions we may have worn in the 90's may not get a pass today. Things are changing all around us and some of us may not know where we fit in. I offer this suggestion from our ancestors, "Don't forget your roots."

WORDS FROM OUR ANCESTORS

Ev'ry time I feel the spirit, moving in my heart, I will pray.

SCRIPTURE: John 4:24(New International Version)

"I WANT JESUS TO WALK WITH ME"

Day Five

DEVOTION

I believe we all have end an goal in mind. No, I'm not just speaking about heaven. I am speaking about our life-long goals and what we have to do to get there. We may plan to live in a certain style house and work toward that goal. We may want a particular car and work toward that goal. We may want to get married and work toward that goal as well. Each of the aforementioned goals is a journey toward something. We don't know what we will face while we are trying to reach our goal, but the goal is still the intended target. We may decide to take someone with us along the journey or decide to travel alone.

Our unknown ancestors believed that life is a journey. According to Bruno Chenu, in his work The Trouble I've Seen:the big book of the Negro Spirituals, he posited, " To speak of movement is to believe, with crazy hope, that the situation is not frozen, that social status is unchangeable. A different future is possible. Nothing would express better the transitional quality of the situation. Tomorrow will be another day, if God is at our side. He further states, "The journey is not an easy one. It is constantly troubled by the attacks of Satan, the symbol of exploitation. One must not be overtaken by the weariness and should travel as lightly as possible. The journey takes on the aspect of a pilgrimage, for it is made in the company of Jesus. But His presence does not make it less rough

There are time in our lives where the journey is rough because of the people who travel with us. There are times where the journey is rough no matter who is traveling with us. Our ancestors recognized their journey toward heaven with Jesus was not going to be an easy, but they wanted to travel the road with Jesus. Our ancestors knew trials weren't going to diminish in this life, but no matter trial they faced, they wanted to Jesus to walk with them.

As we travel this road of life, we have to decide who we take with us. We have to determine who has the ability to hold us when we need to be held, catch us when we fall, and to carry us when we are too weak to carry ourselves. Our unknown ancestors chose Jesus, who do you choose?

WORDS FROM OUR ANCESTORS

I want Jesus to walk with me. I want Jesus to walk with me. All along my pilgrim journey, Lord I want Jesus to walk with me.

SCRIPTURE: John 12:35(New International Version)

"IN DAT GREAT GITTIN' UP MORNING"

Day Six

DEVOTION

It is my personal belief that we all deal with some type of battle between good and evil every day of our lives. I say that because every time we turn on the news, something evil has happened in the world. Some young woman is taken from her home and ends up in a sex trafficking plot. Some young man is gunned down while carrying an iced-tea and a bag of skittles. Some family's home is burned down because of the color of their skin. Some church members are gunned down after a church meeting or the church is burned down after the conclusion of the worship service. The news shows all of the evil that is going on in the world. But the news also shows the good that people do. When a young man is gunned down, protestors rise up and protest over the wrongful death. When the young woman goes missing, organizations rally until the young woman is found. When politicians who do not have the publics issues at the forefront of their elections are up for re-election, someone stands us an runs against them. There is a constant battle between good and evil at work every day of our lives.

Our ancestors believed there will come a time when history will stop and injustice will cease. Our ancestors, according to Bruno Chenu, believed the spirituals' evocation of heaven often has the sweet colors of family reunions or friendship with Jesus. But the dramatic pages of Revelation also our ancestors. Our ancestors believed in the general resurrection and according to Chenu, will take place in this cosmic uproar, and then God would judge humanity. He believed the spirituals that describe this final event sought the conversion of sinners and call all persons to take heed. Our ancestors believed this would take place, "In Dat Great Gittin' Up Mornin.'"

Our ancestors knew there would come a time where injustice would be judged and God would sort everything out. We must have the same belief. We must understand the end will come and God will judge all of us accordingly. We must believe that no matter how much evil is the is in the world, God's justice will prevail and we just have to keep on pressing until "Dat Great Gittin' Up Mornin'" comes.

Words from our Ancestors

Dere's a better day a-coming, Fare you well, Fare you well. O preacher fol' your bible, Fare you well, Fare you well. In dat great gittin' up mornin', Fare you well, Fare you well.

Scripture: 1 Thessalonians 4:16 (New International Version)

"GIVE ME JESUS"

Day Seven

DEVOTION

All of us, who have breath in our bodies, cannot escape death. We can try using all of the age-defying makeup, take all the healthy vitamins and drink as much water as we can, but we are still going to die. None of us know the day, nor the hour death will come knocking, but we can believe it will definitely come knocking. We can spend all of our lives trying to acquire all the wealth in the world, yet death will still come. We can spend the rest of our lives living secluded at the top of a mountain and death will still come. We can become a part of every human-rights organization, give to every charity, build shelters to the homeless and feed the hungry, and we will all still die. Now, this may seem like one may have nothing to live for since death will still come. But this means that no matter what we do in this life, we can expect death to come.

Our ancestors knew that they could not escape death. Our ancestors understood the day would come when they would meet their Maker, so they didn't have time to worry about death. Our ancestors didn't spend their lives worrying about death coming. Our ancestors understood this life was temporary and no matter what this life has to offer, they would rather have Jesus.

We don't know when our lives are going to end, so how we live makes all of the difference in the world. There is nothing that says we can't try to become wealthy or live comfortably. Nothing says that we can't try to get all that life has to offer, but we can't forget about Jesus. We can all try to make as much money as we can, but we must not forget about Jesus. We can all try to purchase many pieces of real estate, but we must not forget about Jesus. Life may offer everything needed to live a good life, but we must not forget about Jesus.

WORDS FROM OUR ANCESTORS

Oh, when I come to die, Give me Jesus. You may have all this world, Give me Jesus.

SCRIPTURE: John 12:21(New International Version)

"GO DOWN MOSES"

Day Eight

DEVOTION

African Americans had to endure slavery during the 17th and 18th centuries. It was during this time where our ancestors worked from sun up to sundown. It was during this time where families were ripped apart and the children of our ancestors were forced to work for free, from an early age. Some of our ancestors were taken into slavery and others were born into slavery. Our ancestors tried to escape and if they were caught, were oftentimes killed. Our ancestors worked hard to make their masters rich. Our ancestors learned about Christianity from their masters and paralleled their lives with the Israelites of the Old Testament. Our ancestors looked at their owners as if they were the Egyptians. They saw themselves as the Israelites. They believed that through divine intervention, God would intervene on their behalf, take care of their oppressors and deliver them from slavery.

For those of us living in the 21st Century, African Americans may not be in slavery anymore, but we still have to fight for freedom. We still have to fight for equal jobs and equal pay. We still have to fight for our children. We still have to fight for our lives. We are still living in a society that was not created for us. We still have to fight back to stay alive and when we do, our lives are on the line. We have to have conversations with our children as to what to do so that they can make it back home safely. Slavery may have ended in the 1800's, but African Americans are still fighting for their freedom.

Down through the years, we have had Dr. Martin Luther King, Jr. try to fight for our freedom. We have had Nat Turner to fight for our freedom. We have had Harriet Tubman fight for our freedom. We have had Fannie Lou Hamer fight for our freedom. Our fight for our freedom didn't end with the Emancipation Proclamation, but it continues to this very day. We have to continue to fight until "Pharaoh" lets our people go. Pharaoh is whatever or whomever is trying to keep us bound. Pharaoh is whatever or whomever is trying to hold our deliverance. We must believe, like our ancestor, that through divine intervention, we will all one day be set free.

WORDS FROM OUR ANCESTORS

Go down Moses, way down in Egypt Land. Tell Old Pharaoh, let my people go.

SCRIPTURE: Exodus 9:1(New International Version)

"I AIN'T GOT WEARY YET"

Day Nine

DEVOTION

How many of us can say, "I ain't got weary yet." I know that I haven't been able to speak those words as of yet in my life, but I believe I am on my way. I believe I am on my way because I believe there is still work that I must do. I believe there are still some places that I must go so that I can help somebody. There are some people I must come in contact with so that I can tell them about Jesus. There are some things that must take place so that I can live out my purpose of helping people live their best lives. I don't believe I can do any of those things if I am weary and worn. I don't believe I can do those things if I don't have the strength to do those things. This is where my faith comes in. My faith allows me to rely on God when I don't feel like I can do on. My allows me to trust in God to live out my purpose in this life. My faith shows me there is more work to do and I can't complain about what needs to be done. This is why I mentioned earlier that I have not spoken the words, "I ain't got weary yet, but I believe I am on my way.

Our unknown ancestors developed a faith in God that sustained them during slavery. Our ancestors were able to hear the stories of the bible and place themselves in the story. It was their faith in God that allowed them to endure the heavy hand of their masters. It was their faith that allowed them to not lose their identity when their masters tried to take everything from them. It was their faith that allowed them to keep pushing, when their bodies were being beaten and worn from working with little to no rest, day in and day out. It's amazing to me that our ancestors were able to speak the words, "I Ain't Weary Yet." There were so many reasons they should have been weary, but the writer or writers of this spiritual had not, at the time of writing this song, reached the point of weariness. The writer recognized there was more that needed to be done and they could not focus on becoming weary. The writer knew if they slowed up work, they may lose their lives, so they didn't have time to focus on being weary.

When there is work to be done, there is no time to get weary. We have to focus on what needs to be done. Yes, we might be tired, weak and worn, but we can't let our focus shift. We have to let our faith be our focus until the work is done.

Words from our Ancestors

I ain't got weary yet, I've been in the wilderness a mighty long time, and I ain't got weary yet.

SCRIPTURE: Galatians 6:9(New International Version)

"NOBODY KNOWS THE TROUBLE I'VE SEEN"

Day Ten

Devotion

There are days that I feel like I am the only one who is going through what I am going through. I feel like I am the only person who is dealing with issues with family, finances and friends. I feel like there is no one else in the world who knows what I have to handle on a daily basis. There are moments I will call my mother and she may give me her advice or stance on things, but at the end of the conversation I don't feel like she fully understands. I call my father and he gives me his advice and stance on the matter at hand as well. But at the end of the conversation, I end up feeling as if he doesn't get where I'm coming from because he doesn't know the troubles I've seen. It is my belief that we have all reached places in our lives where we feel like no one understands our troubles. We have all dealt with issues and we feel like no matter how much we try to articulate our struggles, no one knows the depth of how we feel.

Our unknown ancestors, at one point or another, seemed to have felt this way. Our ancestors must have felt as if no one understood what they were going through. I believe they were able to speak to each other, but they were all in the same situation. Our ancestors seemingly believed no one understood the trouble they've seen, the issues they dealt with, or the problems they had to face. Although it seems like no one understood their plight, they knew persons who understood their situation and that person was Jesus. Our ancestors believed, from their perspective, Jesus knew what they were going through. James Cone, in his work, The Spirituals and the Blues, posits, " If Jesus was not alone his suffering, black slaves were not alone in their oppression under slavery. Jesus was with them! He was God's Black Slave who had come to put an end to human bondage." Our ancestors, in their biblical interpretation, believed that Jesus knew all about their troubles!

Jesus knows all about our troubles. Jesus knows what it is like to be deserted by His friends when He needed them. Jesus knows what it is like to be tempted. There are many other instances where Jesus dealt with the same things we deal with in this 21st Century post-modern urban culture. So, when we feel like no one knows the trouble we've seen, we can believe that Jesus knows all about it.

WORDS FROM OUR ANCESTORS

Nobody knows the trouble I've seen, nobody knows but Jesus.

SCRIPTURE: Hebrews 4:15(New International Version)

"ALL GODS' CHILLUN' GOT A SONG"

Day Eleven

DEVOTION

I remember when I was growing up, when I heard the songs from the 70's and 80's, I knew that was the day to clean. My mom had a record player and when I heard George Clinton, I knew it was time to clean. My mother used those records as a indicator that this was the day to clean. Now, as an adult, when I play Gospel music real loud on a Saturday, my son knows that we are going to spend the morning cleaning the house. I have learned that we all use songs for one reason or another, in our lives. We may have a song in our hearts when we want to be nostalgic. We have a song when we are with our spouse or significant other. We have a song the choir sings that puts us in a place where the only thing that matters at that moment is us and God. We have a song that may speak to our current situation. We may even have a song, like me, that saved our very lives.

Our ancestors were no different. Our ancestors had songs for everything that happened in their lives, from a girl having her first menstrual cycle, to a woman entering into holy matrimony. A song found its place in every day life. Our ancestors knew that they were more than a slave. Bruno Chenu wrote, "But the slave first had to be recognized as a person. The value of a person--the opposite of slavery's degradation--would be expressed by the opulence of the slave's new clothing: the robe, the shoes, the stockings. Everything lacked in the earthly like would be supplied with finery in heaven as symbols of joy offered by God.." Our ancestors knew the song in their hearts spoke of what they couldn't get on earth, but they knew it would be provided to them in heaven. Our ancestors had a song in their hearts and we should too!

What does our song say to us? Does it encourage us? Does it get us to the next leg of the journey? Does it give us what we need to keep on keeping on? We have need to have a song in our hearts and on our lips. Our song should be song, if even for a moment, transports us to a better time. Our song should give us the extra push needed to deal with the vicissitudes of life. Whatever your song is, sing your song because according to our ancestors, "All Gods' Chillun' Got a Song."

WORDS FROM OUR ANCESTORS

I got a song, you got a song, All Gods' Chillun' Got a Song; When I get to heaven, goin to sing a new song, Going to sing all over God's heaven.

SCRIPTURE: Psalm 98:1(New International Version)

"WOKE UP DIS MORNIN'"

Day Twelve

DEVOTION

I have realized over the past couple of years, that I wake up in the morning with my mind on my phone. In this technological age, I seem to rely on my phone more than anything else. I will roll over, open my eyes, turn off my alarm clock and check email. I will then check my Instagram account. Then I check my Facebook account and get caught up on everyone else's life that I missed, while I was sleep. This may sound strange, but I can imagine that many people have the same routine. We go to sleep looking at other peoples' lives and we wake up thinking about the same thing. But I wonder how many people wake up with their minds stayed on Jesus? How many us wake up being thankful for the fact that nothing happened to us last night? How many of us wake up thankful for the fact that our family is still in tact? How many of us wake up thankful for the fact we are still alive? We seem to wake up with everything and everyone else on our mind, except Jesus. We will worry about who posted what on social media instead of the one who took care of us last night.

Our unknown ancestors must have had this mind-frame when they penned this song. Every night must have been a life or death situation because they never knew if they were going to see the morning. Our ancestors had to have their minds stayed on Jesus in order to handle their current situation. Our ancestors didn't have time to hate their neighbor because their mind was stayed on Jesus. Our ancestors didn't have time to think about what happened last night because they woke up with Jesus on their mind. The previous night could have been the last night of their lives. The previous night could have been the night their families were ripped apart. But no matter what happened the night before, they woke up with their mind on Jesus. Our ancestors' current circumstances didn't hinder them from waking up with their minds stayed on Jesus.

When we wake up in the morning with our minds stayed on Jesus, we don't have time to worry about what is going on in the lives of others. When we wake up in the morning with our minds stayed on Jesus, we don't have time to hate our neighbors. We have to make up in our minds that we are going to wake up in the morning with our minds stayed on Jesus.

WORDS FROM OUR ANCESTORS

Woke up Dis' Mornin' wid my min,' and it was stayed, stayed on Jesus. Woke up Dis' Mornin' wid my min,' and it was stayed, stayed on Jesus. Stayed on Jesus, Hallelujah.

SCRIPTURE: Isaiah 26:3(New International Version)

"SWING LOW, SWEET CHARIOT"

Day Thirteen

DEVOTION

I believe that all of us, no matter where we are in life, can't wait for the day we don't have to deal with the troubles of this world. I am not saying that we are all waiting to die. I am saying that I believe that we are waiting for the day where we don't have to deal with things that cause us trouble in this world. I mean, who wants to deal with hurt all of the time? Who wants to deal with heartbreak all of the time? Who wants to deal some form of slavery in the 21st Century? I think that we all want to live in a place where we are delivered and free. We just have to believe that the day is coming. We have to believe that one day our Savior is going to come for us and we are going to meet Him in the air.

Our unknown ancestors waited for the day of emancipation. Our ancestors believed that they were going to be delivered and they would have to travel. Bruno Chenu says, "all of this traveling requires a means of locomotion, for the slaves could not be limited by their capacity to walk." The image of the chariot, according to Chenu, is directly out of the story about the ascension of the prophet Elijah. It is the chariot that comes from heaven and that brings the passenger to heaven. To our ancestor, to go to heaven, was to go home to be with Jesus.

As believers, we are all waiting for the day that we see Jesus. We are waiting for the day that Jesus cracks the sky and calls us to meet Him. This means that we can't stop believing, no matter how hard it gets. We can't stop believing, no matter how difficult things become. We can't throw in the towel just because deliverance doesn't come when we want it come. We have to keep the faith when times get tough. We have to keep the faith when the mountains get too hard to climb. We have to keep the faith and believe that the chariot is coming for us. We have to keep working until the chariot comes. We have to wait until the chariot comes. We have to look out for our neighbor until the chariot comes. We have to keep our eyes on Jesus until the chariot comes.

WORDS FROM OUR ANCESTORS

Swing Low, Sweet Chariot, comin' for to carry me home.

SCRIPTURE: 2 Kings 2:11 (New International Version)

"DIDN'T MY LORD DELIVER DANIEL"

Day Fourteen

Devotion

As a pastor of a Methodist church, I have come in contact with many people who need to be delivered. Deliverance, according to Merriam Webster's Dictionary, is defined as the act of delivering someone or something, or the state of being delivered. When one may speak of deliverance from something, it means there is something or someone that is holding someone else captive. For example, someone could have had a conversation with someone ten years ago and they are still being held captive by the words that were spoken in that conversation. Now, ten years later, those words are still ringing in that person's head and they need to be delivered from that conversation. Or maybe something was done to a person in their past and now that person believes that every person in their present will do the same thing. It can be said that a person needs to be delivered as well. Maybe, someone is suffering from an addiction and the person does not believe they can do without the thing that is seemingly holding them captive. Deliverance is needed in this situation as well. Deliverance comes when the one held in captivity is set free by its captor.

Our unknown ancestors were held captive. Our ancestors were stripped from their homeland forced into free labor. They worked from sun up to down. They were made to believe they were created to be slaves, but they paralleled many stories in the Bible with their own stories. The stories would be heard and internalized. Our unknown ancestors believe the same God that set the Israelites free, would one day come and set them free. Our unknown ancestors believed that deliverance was on the way. We can tell by this particular song, that they believed that God was a Deliverer. This spiritual, in particular, was taken from the story of Daniel in the lion's den. Daniel was a Jewish exile. While Ki Darius was on the throne, a decree was made that no one was to pray to any god or man except for him. The decree was signed and Daniel was thrown into jail. Daniel was found alive in the lion's den. An angel of the Lord was sent to shut the mouths of the lions.

Our ancestors believed that the same God who sent an angel to deliver Daniel from the mouths of the lions would be the same God who would deliver them from their captors. What do you need to be delivered from? Addiction? Past hurt? Past conversation? Abuse? Bad Relationships? Toxic Friendships? Didn't my Lord Deliver Daniel? The good news is that He can deliver you too!

WORDS FROM OUR ANCESTORS

Didn't my Lord deliver Daniel, d'liver Daniel, d'liver Daniel. Didn't my Lord d'liver Daniel, why not every man?

SCRIPTURE: Daniel 6:21-22(New International Version)

"HE NEVER SAID A MUMBLIN' WORD"

Day Fifteen

DEVOTION

I was taught, as a child, to stand up for myself. I should not let anyone walk all over me or take advantage of me. I was taught to make sure that my voice was heard. Over the years my voice became silenced because of various situations. Abuse, divorce, lies, and other things have become the reasons that I have become silent in my latter years. As a father of three African American children, I have taught them to speak when necessary. I know that may sound odd or strange, but in this 21st Century post-modern culture, my children could get locked up or even killed for saying the wrong or right thing. I believe there is a time and a place to speak up and there is a time and a place to say nothing. Sometimes, saying nothing is the best response.

Taken from Chenu's work, "The suffering of Jesus was not ordinary suffering; it was the suffering of the innocent one who was made sport of, who was abandoned and became an apparent failure, who had offered love and been rejected. If Jesus endured everything for the slave's salvation, then the slaves could endure everything for Jesus."

Our ancestors were innocent and did not belong in slavery. They were not prisoners of war. They did not ask to come to America and work for free. They did not ask for the separation of their families. They did not deserve to be treated as 3/5's of a person, but they endured. They endured being sold into slavery. They endured being whipped and mocked. They endured being killed. Our ancestors endured many things during the time of slavery. Our ancestors were able to put their suffering into perspective when they paralleled their suffering to Jesus'

Contrary to popular belief, we don't have to respond to all of the wrong that takes place in our lives. We don't have to respond to the text messages. We don't have to respond to the emails. We don't have to take part in the arguments. We don't have to comment when someone says something negative about us. If Jesus, through all that He went through didn't say a word, from the Garden to the Cross, why do we feel a need to respond to everything? Maybe, just maybe, we can stand still and see the salvation of the Lord!

WORDS FROM OUR ANCESTORS

They crucified my Lord, an' he never said a mumblin' word. Not a word, not a word, not a word.

SCRIPTURE: Isaiah 53:7 (New International Version)

"I WANT TO BE READY"

Day Sixteen

DEVOTION

Many people that I know take a long time to get ready. If I say I will be at their house to pick them up at a certain time, when I get there they are still not ready. Then I have to wait more time until they are finally ready. There have been moments where I told the person the time I was going be there and if they weren't ready, I left. When they came outside and asked my whereabouts, I told them, "You weren't ready, so I left!" Now, when I tell the person I am going to be at a specific place at a specific time, they are ready so that they don't get left again.

We, as believers, are waiting for the day to get caught up to meet the Lord in the air. In the book of Matthew chapter twenty-four, verse forty-four, it says, "So you also must be ready, because the Son of Man will come at an hour when you do not expect him." This passage of scripture teaches us that we must be ready because we don't know the day nor the hour the Son of Man is going to return. How do we get ready? We live the way Christ teaches us to live. We do what Christ teaches us to do. We do what Christ teaches us to do. We work until the work is done, so that we will be ready when He returns.

Our unknown ancestors knew that one day the Lord will come back to get them so they wanted to be ready. They were ready to be delivered from slavery. They were ready to live in bright mansions. They were ready to be at home with their Lord and be free. Our ancestors did not want to be left behind so they kept their eyes on Jesus. Our ancestors kept their eyes toward heaven. Our ancestors kept their eyes on the prize of freedom and they wanted to be like John, who according to the book of Revelation, saw a new heaven and a new earth.

So, we like our ancestors, must be ready when Jesus comes. This means we have to keep our eyes on the work we have been assigned to do. We have to keep our eyes on the Lord. We have to keep alert and awake or we will miss Him when He comes.

WORDS FROM OUR ANCESTORS

I want to be ready, I want to be ready, I want to be ready, to walk in Jerusalem, just like John.

SCRIPTURE: Revelation 21:2 (New International Version)

"IN BRIGHT MANSIONS"

Day Seventeen

DEVOTION

Our ancestors were forced to live in shacks on their master's plantation. They had to share the shack with the bare necessities. They did not live in the best conditions. They had to make the best of what they had until better came along. They taught themselves how to make full meals out of scraps. They hoped for a better tomorrow and believed that tomorrow was on its way.

James Cone writes in his work The Spirituals and the Blues, " Heaven was God's eschatological promise; it was a place of golden streets, pearly gates and the long white robes. There would be no more sadness, no more sorrow and no more hunger-for everybody is goin' feast off'n milk an' honey." For our ancestors, heaven was their home and they were looking forward to going there. James Cone also says, "It was a home indeed, where the slaves would sit down by Jesus, eat at the welcome table, sing and shout, because there would be nobody to turn them out. The black slave took seriously Jesus' promise in the Fourth Gospel that he would prepare a place for them, a place of many mansions."

As believers, we also believe that Jesus went ahead of us to prepare a place for us. The place will be waiting for us. We just have to keep working until we get there. Things may not be going right at the present time, but this is not our home. We may have to deal with broken homes and haters, but this is not our home. We may have to deal with not having enough to eat, but this not our home. We may have to deal with crime infested communities, but this is not our home. There are some things in our lives that we would rather not deal with, but this is not our home. Our home is the place Jesus prepared. Our home is a mansion with many rooms and when He comes back, we will go and be with Him. Our home is a place where we can sing and shout and be with our Lord. We have to keep looking forward to the day when we walk into the front door of our mansions and we hear our Savior say, "Well done, thy good and faithful servant."

WORDS FROM OUR ANCESTORS

In bright mansions above. Lord, I wan't' live up yonder, in bright mansions above.

SCRIPTURE: John 14:2-3(New International Version)

"JUST A CLOSER WALK WITH THEE"

Day Eighteen

DEVOTION

One day as I was traveling, I caught a flat tire. I didn't have a spare tire and I was on my way to an important meeting. I thought I had AAA, but it had expired the previous year. I sat there trying to figure out what to do. Then I remembered that my automobile insurance came with roadside assistance. I called the insurance company, told them my issue and my location, and within the hour, someone came, changed my tire and I was able to make my meeting. See, I thought I was able to use AAA, but that was not available to me at the time. Things were rough because I had a flat tire and had no way of changing it myself. My insurance company way there the whole time, even when I didn't immediately realize it.

We must remember that things are going to happen in this life at the most inopportune time. We could be on our way somewhere and the car breaks down. Our rent or mortgage is due and something comes out of our account that we did not expect. We start a new job and end up getting hurt. We can't always stop things from happening to us on our journey, in life. But we as believers must remember who we have traveling with us.

Our ancestors wanted Jesus to walk with them, no matter how far they had to walk. they recognized that Jesus knew all about their troubles, so who better to walk with them. Our ancestors believed that Jesus could handle and take care of anything they had to handle in this life. Our ancestors wanted to walk with Jesus as close as possible, even if their current condition made it look as if Jesus wasn't there.

Who we have traveling with us in the life makes all the difference in the world! There may be times we think we are able to count on one thing to help us and that thing is not there. We can't be bent out of shape, but we must remember there is one who sticks closer than a brother. There is one who told his disciples and it still rings true today, "I will never leave you nor forsake you. I will be with you always, even until the end of the age. We have to remember that He is always there no matter the circumstance. We must all desire a closer walk with Him. This is the only way we will get through this life.

WORDS FROM OUR ANCESTORS

Just a closer walk with thee. Grant it Jesus, it my plea. Daily walking close to Thee, let it be dear Lord, let it be.

SCRIPTURE: Hosea 11:12(New International Version)

"STANDIN' IN THE
NEED OF PRAYER'

Day Nineteen

DEVOTION

Every Sunday, when it is time to open the altar for prayer, I ask the question, "How many people believe that prayer changes things?" Many of the congregants either raise their hands and shout Amen. I ask this question for several reasons. The first reason I ask this question is that it serves as a reminder. I believe that sometimes we need to be reminded about the power of prayer. We didn't ask our parents for something that we wanted if we didn't believe they had the power to grant our request. We asked for what we wanted because we believed. Another reason I ask the question is that I believe we need to be reminded that we can trust God with everything that we go through and deal with in our lives. Some of us will run to social media before we run to God. Some of us will run to our spouses or significant others before we run to God. Some of us will run to other things before we run to God. God seems to be the last one we run to when we have to handle the issues of life. I read somewhere, "Prayer is to the Christian, what oxygen is to the human." We need prayer to survive." If that is the case, why don't we pray more? Why don't more people believe in the power of prayer?

Our ancestors believed in the power of prayer, even if their circumstances didn't immediately change. Our ancestors kept on praying because they knew one day their change was going to come. The same way we didn't stop making our requests known to our parents until we got an answer, is the same way we need to pray to God. Prayer does not mean that things are going to change immediately. Prayer means that we trust in the one who has the power to change our situation.

When we are going through the trials of life, it's okay to pray. When we have done all that we know to do, it's okay to pray. When we are feeling the pressures of life, it's okay to pray. No one can tell your story like you. No one knows what you are going through like you. No one can explain your problem like you. Our ancestors went to the Lord on their own behalf and the good news is that you can too!

WORDS FROM OUR ANCESTORS

It's me, it's me, it's me Oh Lord, standing in the need of prayer.

SCRIPTURE: Psalm 39:12(New International Version)

"WE'LL STAND THE STORM"

Day Twenty

DEVOTION

When I was in Wilberforce, Ohio in 2011, I remember that it started to snow. Now being from Philadelphia, I am accustomed to all types of storms, or at least I thought was! It started to snow and I thought I was going to be okay. I had dealt with storms before. Then I heard a sound hitting my car harder than snow, so I thought it was hail. I had been through hail. Then my friend, who was in the car with me, told me that it wasn't hail, but it was in fact an ice storm. Yes, ice was hitting the car! I had never dealt with an ice storm before and I actually started to panic. Although I had dealt with storms in the past and present, I had never been in an ice storm. My friend told me that Ohio dealt with ice storms all of the time in the winter and to drive carefully. I drove as slow as I could, but I was scared the entire time. My friend put me at ease and told me, "It's okay, it won't last long and we will be fine". To my surprise, the ground was covered with ice, but the storm didn't last long and at the end of it all, we were fine. We had withstood the storm.

Our ancestors had to deal with storms as well. Storms of racism. Storms of sexism. Storms of classicism. Storms of abuse. Storms of separation and the list could go on and on. Although they had to deal with the storms, they too realized the storm was not going to last. They knew the storm would pass. They knew whatever storm they had to face would be over soon. This allowed them to be able to deal with the storm. this allowed them to handle the elements of the storm. This allowed them to to make due until the storm passed. They learned how to move in the storm. They learned how to take care of each other in the storm. They learned how to wade in the water. The storms they had to go through didn't stop them from waiting until the storm ended. Our ancestors never gave up trying to escape to freedom. Our ancestors never gave up looking out for each other. Our ancestors did not stop trying to make it out of the storms in their lives.

We will all face storms in our lives and our storms may be different. But just like ice storms, hail storms, thunderstorms and the other unnamed storms, they won't last long. This means we can't give up when we are faced with a storm. We can't give in when we are faced with a storm. We have to prepare as best we can for when the storms come. Some storms we can't prepare for, but we must learn how to deal with them once we are in them. We may have to take it slow, but we can't stop moving. We may have to find shelter, but we can't stop moving. We may have to enlist the aid of our neighbors, but we can't stop moving. The storms in life didn't stop our ancestors and since we are our ancestors wildest dreams, we can't let the storms of life stop us.

WORDS FROM OUR ANCESTORS

Oh! stand the storm, it won't be long. We'll anchor by and by. Stand the storm, it won't be long, we'll anchor by and by.

SCRIPTURE: Isaiah 43:1-2-(New International Version)

"WE'VE COME
A LONG WAY, LORD"

Day Twenty-One

DEVOTION

If I had the time, I would tell my story. I would tell of all the things I made it through. I would tell of all the traps I didn't fall in. I would tell of all the doors I was able to walk through and all of the windows God has opened. In my forty years of living, I can tell a story of how God was and is involved in the details of my life. I believe that all of us have a story to tell. We can all tell of things we went through, miracles we've seen, windows we've seen open, and the ways that God has made in our lives. We can look back over our lives and see the handprint of God. Things were not always the way we wanted them to be, but we made it. Things didn't always turn out the way we wanted them to turn out, but we made it. People weren't always there when we wanted them there, but we made it. There are some opportunities we missed, but we made it.

Our unknown ancestors knew who to give credit to when it came to their lives. Our ancestors made it through the Mid-Atlantic slave trade. Our ancestor made it through the night. Our ancestors made it through the Underground Railroad. Our ancestors made it through the whippings. Our ancestors made it through the long days. Our ancestors made it through the auction blocks. Our ancestors made it through being taken from their homelands. Our ancestors made it through four hundred years of being slaves. Our ancestors gave credit to God . Our ancestors knew it was God who kept. Our ancestors knew it was God who kept them in the burning heat. Our ancestors knew it was God who kept them when they tried to escape. Our ancestors knew it was God who brought them from a mighty long way.

How do I know? We are here to tell their story. We are here to keep their memories alive. We are here to pay homage to them. We are here to let their voices be heard, even in this 21st Century. We can look at their lives and know it was only God who brought them out. We have to be able thank God that we are still here. We have to be able to thank God that no matter what has come our way, God is still orchestrating the details of our lives. We can all thank God that we've come a mighty long way.

WORDS FROM OUR ANCESTORS

We've come a long way, Lord, a mighty long way, we've borne our burdens in the heat of the day. But we know the Lord had made the way, we've come long way, Lord, a mighty long way.

SCRIPTURE: Deuteronomy 1:31 (New International Version)

"OVER MY HEAD, I HEAR MUSIC IN THE AIR"

Day Twenty One

DEVOTION

Bruno Chenu posits, " ...the spirituals are songs of faith. They consider God to be the ultimate goal in the journey of faith, but they are not theological treatises...for the slave, music and song constituted proofs of the existence of God." Our ancestors, in this song did not doubt the existence of God because the spirituals are songs of faith. W. E. B. Dubois writes in his work, The Souls of Black Folks, " through all the sorrow of the songs of the Sorrow Songs, there breathes a hope-a faith in the ultimate justice of things. The minor cadences of despair change often to triumph and calm confidence. Sometimes it is faith in life, sometimes faith in death, sometimes faith in assurance of boundless justice in some fair world beyond." He further writes, "Even so is the hope that sang in the songs of my fathers well sung. If somewhere in this whirl and chaos of things there dwells Eternal Good, pitiful yet masterful, then anon in His good time America shall rend the Veil and the prisoned shall go free." Our ancestors did not stop believing that there was a God somewhere. Our ancestors did not give up hope that there must be a God somewhere. Our ancestors did not give into their circumstances and doubt that there was a God somewhere. They continued to sing. They continued to point their faces toward the rising sun. They continued to believe their songs would reach wherever God was and He would one day set them free.

We, like our ancestors, must believe that there is a God somewhere. A God who still opens the eyes of the blind. A God who still performs miracles. A God who still sets the captives free. This means that we can't stop looking to God. We can't stop looking to God to perform miracles in our lives. We can't stop having faith in God that He will deliver His children from the hand of the enemy. We can't stop hoping that God show up and show out. We can't stop believing that wherever God may be, He is still watching over us and one day, He will come for us and we will be with Him.

WORDS FROM OUR ANCESTORS

Over my head I hear music in the air. There must be a God somewhere.

SCRIPTURE: Revelation 14:2(New International Version)

"MY GOD IS A ROCK IN A WEARY LAND"

Day Twenty-Two

DEVOTION

As I continue to grow and mature, I have realized that no day is like the next. There are day when things go right and everything seems to be right in my world. Then there are days when it seems as if all hell is breaking loose and nothing is going right. Every time I turn on the news there seems to be something that goes wrong in the world. Someone seems to lose their life over something minute. The government is at odds with itself. Days like these makes you feel as if you want to skip a day or two. Days like this make you feel like you want to go back in time, when things were seemingly better. Days like these make you ask the question, "Why do we have to have days like this?" Days like these can throw us into a rut, if we let it. But then I remember that days are not always going to be like this. Times are not always going be like these and we have to continue forward to better days. These are the times in which we realize God is a shelter in the time of storm.

Our unknown ancestors experienced times like these, as well. There were times when family members were sold off to another plantation. There were times when fellow slaves would not make it through the night. There were times when the days seemed longer and the nights seemed shorter. There is no particular time, rhyme, or reason that has been gathered as to why this particular song was written. But for whatever reason, our ancestors believed their God was a rock in a weary land. Our ancestors believed that even in a world that was not their own, even in a culture in which they had to adapt, God was still their shelter. God was there to take care of them. God was their to cover them. God was there for them in their weariness. Despite all our ancestors had to deal with, they were confident knowing that God was there to protect them.

We must be confident that in this life, God is a shelter in our land. We must understand that no matter how unstable the world is God is stable. No matter how uncomfortable the world may seem, God is still a God of comfort.

WORDS FROM OUR ANCESTORS

My God is rock in a weary land, a weary land, a weary land. My God is a Rock in a weary land, a shelter in the time of storm.

SCRIPTURE: Isaiah 32:2 (New International Version)

"OH, FIX ME"

Day Twenty Three

When I was about sixteen, I used to get stomach aches from out of nowhere. I mean the pain would be so unbearable, I would have to stay out of school for days. I started going to specialists and no one could figure out what was wrong. I remember walking into the last office of the specialist and simply said the words, "Fix Me!" I had been to doctor after doctor and I wanted the pain to go away. I wanted to be released from the pain and nothing that was prescribed from the previous doctors worked. I just wanted the last specialist to fix me. I had an issue that I couldn't get rid of. I had to live through this pain and I just wanted to be done with the pain. How many others feel like I felt? People try all sorts of medications and home remedies. People can run the gamut of things they want changed in their lives and to say it as plainly as I can, they want their issues fixed.

Our ancestors, on their pilgrim journey, wanted Jesus to walk with them. They understood the only One who would help them along the way was Jesus. It was Jesus who could lead them home. It was Jesus who understood their plight. It was Jesus who would travel with them every step of the way. And our ancestors believed it was Jesus who could fix them. Jesus could fix them as they walked. Jesus could fix them as they traveled. Jesus could heal their bodies so they didn't have to rely on anything else to help them as they traveled toward heaven.

We have to know who to go to when we need help. We can go to the podiatrist when we have a foot problem. We can go to the optometrist when we have an eye problem. We can go to an ear, nose and throat doctor when we are having an issue with our ears , our nose or our throat. But when these doctors can't help us fix our issue, we can go to Jesus and say "Fix me." We can ask Jesus to fix our issues. We can ask Jesus to fix our circumstances. We can ask Jesus to fix us for our journey toward heaven. All we have to do is say, Fix me, Jesus, fix me.

WORDS FROM OUR ANCESTORS

Oh, Fix me. Oh, Fix Me Oh, Fix Me. Fix me Jesus, fix me.

SCRIPTURE: 1 John 1:9 (New International Version)

"OH FREEDOM"

Twenty-Four

DEVOTION

One of my undergraduate professors said something profound that still rings true to me today. He said, "Offense is the spirit of entrapment. Once a person has offended you, they have your mind." He let us know that once you have a persons's mind, you can get them to do whatever you want them to do. Even Harriet Tubman said, " I freed three thousand slaves and I would have freed more if they only knew they were slaves."

As we look at our unknown ancestors, we must understand that there were some who accepted the fact they were slaves. There were some who accepted their fate and worked until they died. But just like our song says for today, "Before I be a slave, I'll be buried in my grave and go home to my Lord and be free." There were some who did not believe in the idea of slavery. There were some who believed that there was more to life than their present circumstance. There were many who escaped to freedom via the Underground Railroad because they knew freedom was waiting for them. They knew that they were not created to be slaves. They knew that even though their bodies were enslaved, their minds were free.

How many us have been enslaved in our minds by something? We think that we can't live without something or someone. We have succumbed to the pressures of life. We have given up to our present circumstances. We have thrown our hands up and let life have its way with us. If anyone of us have fallen into any of these categories, we must believe there can be freedom. We must believe that if we find ourselves entrapped or enslaved in our bodies, for whatever reasons, our minds can still be free.

WORDS FROM OUR ANCESTORS

Oh Freedom, oh freedom. Oh freedom over me. And before I be a slave, I'll be buried in by grave, and go home to my Lord and be free.

SCRIPTURE: 2 Corinthians 3:17 (New International Version)

"I GOT A NEW NAME"

Day Twenty-Five

DEVOTION

When we are born, most of the time we are given a name. We are given a name from our parents, grandparent, older siblings or anyone else who has been given the task in naming us. When I was born, my mother said she took one look at me and gave me both of my names. She said I looked like both of my names. As I grew older, there were moments that I didn't like one or both of my names because I didn't feel like they were descriptive of my nature. After some time, I saw that my mom was right and I decided that I like both of my names and wanted to keep them. People may shorten my name or call me some derivative of name, but my name is my name. No one can take it from me because it's mine.

Our ancestors were brought over to America from the west coast of Africa. They were from different tribes and forced to work together. When they were purchased by their owners, they were given new names. The names they were given signified who "owned" them. The names they were given at birth were more than likely never used again in their new world. But as ones who believed in heaven and believed they were going there, they believed they would be given a new name. They believed the angels would change their names, once they reached Zion. They believed that once their name was changed in heaven, no one would be able to take it from them.

What's in a name? A name, as defined by Webster's Merriam dictionary, is defined as a word or set of words by which a person, animal, place, or thing is known, addressed, or referred to. We name our children, our pets, our cars, our streets, our highways and many other things in this life to identify those persons, places or things. Sometimes names will be changed for a number of reasons. Although our ancestors had their name changed here on Earth, they knew one day they would get a new name and nothing would be able to change that. The name change would signify that they made it to heaven. The name change would mean their earthly masters had nothing to do with it. The masters could not change it because their name was now given by their new Master. Our ancestors would be able to keep their new name because their locale would not change anymore.

One day when we get to glory, our names are going to change. What will you new name be?

WORDS FROM OUR ANCESTORS

I got a new name over in Zion, and it's mine, mine, mine.

SCRIPTURE: Revelation 2:17 (New International Version)

"I COULDN'T HEAR NOBODY PRAY"

Day Twenty-Six

———————•◆•———————

DEVOTION

When I was sixteen, I had a bad asthma attack. I was hospitalized for a week. While I was in the hospital, I was diagnosed with the flu and bronchitis. My heart rate dropped so low that I was immediately admitted into the Intensive Care Unit. There were doctors coming to my room around the clock to check on me. I didn't know how close I was to dying. There were moments I felt alone. There were moments I felt like there was nothing else the doctors could do. There were moments I didn't want to see anymore doctors. There were moments I didn't know what was going on. There were moments I didn't want any visitors. One night, in the middle of the night, I thought, "I couldn't hear nobody pray".

Our ancestors had to endure the Mid-Atlantic slave trade. There was no singing about the happenings of the day. There was no singing about the chief's daughter getting married. There were no songs about the youngest daughter of the tribe getting her menstrual and becoming a woman. There were sounds of moaning. There were sounds of weeping. There were sounds of crying. There were sounds of wailing. Our ancestors were packed on the ships. It was during these moments it was said that our ancestors wrote this song. It was during these moments that it would seem like no one could be heard praying, but it does not mean that no one was praying, the words of the prayer were just not heard. This song seemingly moves from our ancestors feeling alone, to the chilly waters of the Atlantic Ocean, to the valley and then finally to their trouble being over.

As I was in the Intensive Care Unit, I couldn't hear nobody pray, but that didn't stop me from praying. It didn't stop me from believing that things would eventually change, even though I had a moment I felt like I was by myself. If you find yourself in a moment where you can't hear nobody pray, don't stop praying. Don't stop believing. If you find yourself in the chilly waters of life, don't stop looking to Jesus. If you find yourself in the valley of the shadow of death, don't stop pressing toward heaven because one day you will be able to shout the word Hallelujah from the rooftops because your trouble will be over.

Words from our Ancestors

An' I couldn't hear nobody pray O Lord, I couldn't hear nobody pray, O Lord. O' way down yonder by myself, I couldn't hear nobody pray.

Scripture: Matthew 26:40 (New International Version)

"LORD I WANT TO BE A CHRISTIAN"

Day Twenty-Seven

DEVOTION

When I first entered the preaching ministry, my former pastor told me, "Don't be like anyone else, be like you because God already called them. Now He's called you." As I continued in the ministry, I started looking at different styles of preaching and how people were responding to those styles of preaching. I started to say to myself, " I wanted to sound like that and I want people to respond like that!" As time progressed, I began to realize that no matter how many times I tried to imitate others, the response may not always be the same. I realized the style of preaching exhibited by others did not fit me and I had lost my own voice. I spoke to one of my mentors one day and they told me, "Stop trying to be like everyone else and be like you. Let the people see you when you stand behind the sacred desk. You'll be more comfortable when you do." When I internalized what was said at the beginning of my ministry and what was said in the not-so distant past, I realized that I have to be the best me I could be and the only way I could do that was to be myself. I couldn't worry about how I was viewed by others. I had to be comfortable with me and be comfortable in that moment because if I was going to emulate anyone at that moment, it was going to be Jesus. If I was going to imitate anyone in that moment, it was going to be Jesus. If I was going to try and be like anyone, I was going to be like Jesus.

Our ancestors didn't want to be like their masters, they didn't even want to be like each other, but they wanted to be like Jesus. Our ancestors wanted to be a Christian in their hearts despite how they were treated. Our ancestors wanted to be more holy in their hearts despite what was going on around them. Our ancestors decided that if they were going to emulate or imitate, they were going to emulate and imitate Jesus.

I heard someone say, "Imitation is the best flattery." When we decide to imitate someone, we follow the good they do as well as the bad. We follow what they do to the letter. It's like the game, "Follow the Leader." You win the game when you do everything the leader does. You lose the game if you try to do one thing, but the leader does something else. If we want to live this life to the fullest, we have to choose the right person to follow. We have to choose the right person to imitate. Who do you want to be like?

WORDS FROM OUR ANCESTORS

Lord, I want to be a Christian in my Heart

SCRIPTURE: Matthew 6:21 (New International Version)

"I KNOW THE LORD HAS LAID HIS HAND ON ME"
Day Twenty-Eight

DEVOTION

Our ancestors believed in the preaching, teaching and healing of Jesus. They believed the stories of the scriptures where persons were healed because they were touched by Jesus, i.e., the blind man who was told to wash in the pool of Siloam and the woman with the issue of blood. In the first mentioned story, the man was told to put mud on his eyes and wash in the pool seven times. In the latter story mentioned, the woman pressed her way to Jesus until she was able to touch the hem of His garment. In each of these stories, the persons personally interacted with the Lord and were healed of their infirmities. Our ancestors believed that if the stories in the Bible are true, Jesus had the power to heal them as well. Jesus had the power to make them whole. Jesus had the power to heal them of all infirmities. Jesus could change their total situation.

When things happen in our lives, we have to know who helped us. We have know who healed us. We have to know who turned our situations around. It's one things to be healed of any infirmity, and another thing to have our minds be made whole in the process. In the story with the woman with the issue of blood, when she was healed, Jesus asked, "Who touched me?" Jesus knew this was a different type of touch because He felt power and virtue come out of Him. When the woman revealed herself, Jesus told her, " Your faith has made you whole." There is a difference between being healed and being made whole. We can be healed, but not be made whole. When we go through things in life, we may lose some things along the way. We may lose friends, we may lose finances and we may lose fellowship. The woman lost finances because the bible says she lost all that she had. She lost fellowship because of her illness. She needed to be made whole because of what she lost in her twelve year moment of sickness. She needed restoration to take place in her life. She was restored because despite her condition, she owned up to what she did. She did not cower back into the crowd because she got what she needed from Jesus. She did not blame the touch on somebody else. She wanted the Lord to know who touched Him because she knew it was because of Him that she was healed. In turn, Jesus gave her so much more.

When the Lord does something for us in our lives, we have to know it was the Lord. The medicine may have helped, but it was the Lord. The creditor may have given a reprieve, but it was the Lord. We have to give credit where credit it due.

WORDS FROM OUR ANCESTORS

I know the Lord, I know the Lord, I know the Lord has laid His hands on me.

SCRIPTURE: Psalm 139:5 (New International Version)

"I NEVER INTEND TO DIE IN EGYPT LAND"

Day Twenty-Nine

DEVOTION

Cone suggests in his work, entitled The Spirituals and the Blues, that "the black experience in America is a history of servitude and resistance, or survival in the land of death. It is a story of black life in chains and what that meant for the souls and bodies of black people."He goes on further to assert that this is the experience that created the spirituals, and it must be recognized if we are to render a valid theological interpretation of these songs. Cone argues that the divine liberation of the oppressed from slavery is the central theological concept in the black spirituals.

Our ancestors equated their lives with the lives of the Israelites. They believed, as stated in an earlier devotion that they were not created to be slaves and that they were created to be free. This meant that if deliverance was not going to come immediately, it would come eventually. This also meant that gathering for worship services was not just for the worship of God, but also for meeting to plan ways of escape from the hands of the slave masters and a new life outside of the plantation. This also meant our ancestors had to hold to the belief that freedom was theirs. They knew they weren't created to live and die on the plantation. This meant that although their bodies were enslaved, their minds were free to hold on to the thought of freedom.

We have all been through situations that were seemingly meant for our downfall. We have been in situations where it may have felt like the situation was created for our downfall or even our death. But we must realize although situations may look deathly, it does not have to result in death. Cone suggests even further that the basic idea of the spirituals is that slavery contradicts God; it is a denial of God's will. To be enslaved is to be declared nobody, and that form of existence contradicts God's creation to people to be God's children. Because black people believed that they were God's children, they affirmed their somebodiness, refusing to reconcile their servitude with divine revelation. Cone also states that the message of liberation in the spirituals is based on the biblical contention that God's righteousness is revealed in deliverance of the oppressed from the shackles of human bondage. That message was an expression of the slave's confidence that can be trusted to stand by God's Word… the slave firmly believed that "God would make a way out of no way," meaning that God's providential care of God's children cannot be thwarted by white masters.

Don't let your situation be the death of you! Don't intend to die in Egypt!

WORDS FROM OUR ANCESTORS

Lord, I can't stay away, Lord I can't stay away. I don't never intend to die in Egypt Land

---

SCRIPTURE: Psalm 118:17

"I HAVE ANOTHER BUILDING"

Day Thirty

DEVOTION

Our ancestors were made to pile up in shacks on the master's plantation. The living conditions were not conducive to good health, but our ancestors were able to survive. Our ancestor's bodies were racked with pain and they still were made to work in the heat of the day. Hands were blistered and calloused, but they still had to work. Legs were bruised because of the tedious work of picking cotton, but they still had to work. Our ancestors got pregnant and were not taken to the hospital. They had their children and were right back to work immediately. To make matters worse, when the children became of age, were forced to work as well. But our ancestors looked forward to the day when they would go to a building not made by hands. They looked forward to the day they would not have to deal with picking cotton. They looked forward to the day when they didn't have to listen to the slave masters because they would be with "The Master."

Many people spend most of their lives working. They work from the time they get out of the bed in the morning until their heads hit the pillow, at night. They work anywhere from eight hours a day to twenty hours a day depending on the work. Bodies are falling apart because of the work.

Hands are blistered because of the work. Feet are calloused because of the work. Families are split apart because of the work. Health is failing because of the work. The onset of sickness may take place because of the work. And all of this just happens to our bodies. Our minds are working as well. How are we going to pay our bills? How are we going to feed our families? How are we going to get to work in the morning? How are we going to raise the budget for the church? How are we going to raise the budget for our individual households? Our minds seem to be working just as much as our bodies! But the good news is that all the work we have done, are doing and will do won't last always. Our bodies may be deteriorating every day, but soon and very soon we will get new bodies. We won't have to deal with sickness. We won't have to deal with pain. We won't have to deal with hurt. We won't have to deal with suffering. We won't have to deal with the roof leaking. We won't have to deal with the heater bursting. We won't have to deal with the foundation our our homes caving in. We can look forward to a time when we will have a mansion in heaven with the Lord. We can look forward to a time when we will shed this body of flesh and put on a robe of glory and we will be able to tell the story of how we made it over.

Words from our Ancestors

I know I have another building. I know it's not made with hands. I want to go to Heaven and I want to go right. O, I want to go to Heaven all robed in white.

Scripture: 2 Corinthians 5:1 (New International Version)

HE'S GOT THE WHOLE WORLD IN HIS HANDS

Day Thirty-One

DEVOTION

When I was growing up, I remember learning the song, "He's got the whole world in His hands." I didn't think of the song on a theological level, but I think about it on the child's level. I started thinking that everything that is in the world is in God's hands?! You mean that the mountains are in His hands, Yes! You mean the oceans are in His hands, Yes! You mean the bird and the bees are in His hands, Yes! You mean the animals on the ground and under the ground are in His hands too, Yes!!! I then said to myself, "If al of these things are in His hands, then how big are God's hands?" My simple conclusion as a child was, "they are big enough to hold it all!" Then as an adult, I read Psalm 24:1 and it confirmed the words of the song I had learned as a child. It read, "The earth is the Lord's and the fullness thereof. The world and they that dwell therein." This verse has impacted my life because God's hands are so big they can hold everything in the world and delicate enough to take care of me! This is so amazing that God is so big and yet so personal.

Our ancestors recognized this fact as well. Our ancestors not only knew that God had the whole world in His hands, but the slave master was in His hands. The liar was in His hands. The gambler was in His hands. Anyone they could think of was in God's hands. This meant that they could put themselves in the hands of God. Even Jesus said from the cross, "Into thy hands, I commit my spirit." This suggests that no matter what is going on in the world, it is still in the hands of God. Our hurt, is in the hands of God. Our pain is in the hands of our God. Our heartache is in the hands of God. Our heartbreak is in the hands of God. Our suffering is even in the hands of God. So we can take solace in the fact that there is nothing in this world that is not in the hands God because He's got the whole world in His hands.

WORDS FROM OUR ANCESTORS

He's got the whole world, in His hand. He's got the whole world, in His hands. He's the whole world, in His hands. He's got the whole world in His hands.

SCRIPTURE: Psalm 24:1 (New International Version)
